MW01166426

MONSTER MACHINES

JAPANESE BULLET TRAIN

John Bankston

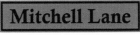

Mitchell Lane
PUBLISHERS

2001 SW 31st Avenue
Hallandale, FL 33009
www.mitchelllane.com

First Edition, 2020.

Author: John Bankston
Designer: Ed Morgan
Editor: Lisa Petrillo

Little Mitchie is an imprint of Mitchell Lane Publishers.

Names/credits:
Title: Arctic Japanese Bullet Train / by John Bankston
Description: Hallandale, FL :
Mitchell Lane Publishers, [2020]

Series: Monster Machines
Library bound ISBN: 9781680204544
eBook ISBN: 9781680204551

Contents

Chapter 1

An Olympic Feat

The Olympics were coming to Tokyo. The bullet train wasn't ready.

Japan lay in ruins after World War II. Bombs had destroyed much of the country's largest city, Tokyo. The country slowly rebuilt. By the 1960s, there were new factories and gleaming apartment towers.

Yoshinori Sakai at the opening ceremony of the 1964 Olympics.

In 1964, Tokyo was set to host the Olympic Games. The country could show the world how much it had changed. The train was part of that.

The bullet train was named for the engine's sharp nose. It looked like something from *The Jetsons*, the popular futuristic cartoon show. The train was more than the engine and the cars it pulled. The Japanese called it "shinkansen" or "new main line." The line needed special tracks which were laid over three hundred miles between Tokyo and Japan's second-largest city, Osaka.

The Japanese government could not force people to sell their land. Tracks cut away from a straight route. Rivers and canals were paved over. The train ran on electricity. Power lines were strung over tracks.

Work began in 1959. The new train was supposed to cost one billion dollars. After five years of construction, it cost twice that.

This super fast train is named for its bullet-shaped nose.

On the morning of October 1, 1964 a huge crowd waited. At six a.m. the first bullet train sped into Tokyo Station. It was on time.

"It was like flying in the sky; it was that kind of feeling," Fumihiro Araki, one of the first railway engineers, told a reporter from the *Los Angeles Times*. "On a clear day, you could see Mt. Fuji. It felt like you were sailing above the sea."

The project changed the country. It began because one man was afraid that trains would disappear.

FAST FACT

A Japanese bullet train is allowed to be only 15 seconds late or early to its destination. Today as many as 13 trains per hour travel along the bullet train's first line in each direction.

Chapter 2

Speed Dreams

Trains were disappearing. In the United States, steam-powered **locomotives** once traveled at more than 100 miles per hour. By the 1950s, highways criss-crossed the country. Cars sped people to jobs and schools. Fewer people rode trains.

By the 1950s, more people in Japan were also using cars. Shinji Sogo ran Japanese National Railways (JNR). He wanted to save the railroad. In 1957, an engineer showed him how.

Sogo watched Hideo Shima connect a railway car to electricity. Power traveled from a motor on the **axles** to the wheels. It went very fast. Sogo wondered what would happen if a train could go twice as fast as a car? Wouldn't more people take the train to save time?

Japan is made up of a chain of islands. The whole country is about the size of California. Because of its many mountains, there are fewer places where people can live. Most Japanese live in cities.

Today 35 million people live around Tokyo. Before the bullet arrived, trains made the trip between it and Osaka in seven hours. Cars were even slower.

Sogo hired Shima to work at JNR. They hoped to build a train that would speed passengers between the cities in just four hours.

FAST FACT

Today the average ticket for a bullet train ride costs $130.

Chapter 3

Better Travel

Bullet trains helped Tokyo grow. The trains connected smaller towns to the huge city. People could live further from work because bullet trains got them home faster than if they drove.

A bullet train in Tokyo

It also helped businesses. Large businesses have the money to buy supplies from far away. Smaller businesses couldn't connect with distant cities. Now, opportunities are just a bullet train away.

Anytime a new line is built, people move into homes near stations. New businesses open as well.

Before the bullet train, many Japanese traveled by car. The train is safer. No one has ever died in a bullet train accident. It has never derailed.

Since 1964, the country has faced earthquakes, typhoons, and even volcanic eruptions. The bullet keeps passengers safe. Early warning systems stop the train before earthquakes hit. It has continued running in storms when cars could not. Because it does not pollute as much as a car, it may have made the air easier to breath.

FAST FACT

In June of 2018, the Hello Kitty bullet train began running. It is named for the popular cartoon character. Connecting the west and south, the Kitty train runs between Shin-Osaka Station and Hakata Station in Fukuoka. Its first two cars are pink and white with pictures of Kitty. In the second car, people can take selfies with a Kitty statue.

Chapter 4

Train Tech

High-speed rail happened because of a problem. Before the 1960s, trains in Japan ran on tracks made to handle mountain travel. Its gauge was narrow. Gauge is the space between the outer rails of a track. Back then, it was three and one half foot wide.

Wider train tracks were needed to keep the train flat at high speeds.

This thin gauge was perfect for slow travel along a mountain. But faster trains needed wider tracks. Japan would have to build new ones, and make them more than one foot wider. The new tracks were placed away from rail crossings and traffic. They stayed on flat surfaces.

In the U.S., passenger and freight trains share tracks. They often stop. This makes them very slow. The country's fastest trains rarely go over 100 mph.

Japan's bullet train is much faster. This is because electricity is sent to each wheel from a 185 kilowatt traction motor connected to the axle. Power comes from 25 kilovolt ac overhead lines. This is like a streetcar, an above-ground vehicle that transports people like buses except the tracks are smoother and built right into the streets. Both streetcars and bullet trains are connected to pantographs, a jointed framework carrying electric **current** from the overhead wires. The famous bullet shape cuts down on wind resistance, which also helps it move faster.

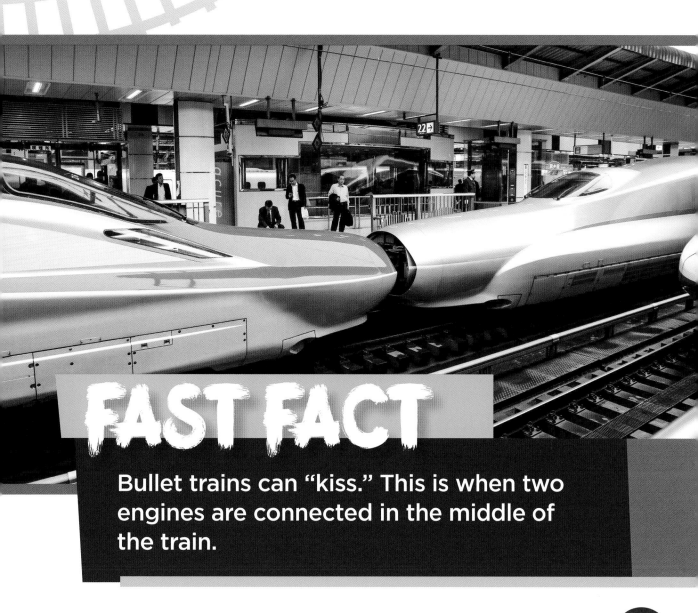

FAST FACT

Bullet trains can "kiss." This is when two engines are connected in the middle of the train.

Chapter 5

Need for Speed

When Japan's bullet train began running in 1964, no train in the world was faster. In Europe, the fastest trains went 90 mph. The first bullet hit 130 mph. Today the trains average 170 mph. In China, high-speed trains approach an average of 190 mph.

Speeding into a rail station is the Shinkansen, the Japanese term for the bullet train system.

Yet Japan's bullet has broken more than speed records. The very first line is the busiest in the world. Every year, more than 160 million passengers board the train. After more than 50 years in service, it is approaching 6 *billion* passengers. More than 10 billion people have ridden on Japan's high-speed rail system.

A Maglev train uses magnets to 'float' the train for speed and smoother rides.

Japanese trains are breaking speed records. A new Maglev train hit 374 mph—a world record. Maglev stands for magnetic levitation. The tracks are in the ground and work like two repelling magnets, causing the trains to float over a guideway. The ride is fast, and smooth. When it is completed, it is expected to carry passengers from Tokyo to Osaka in only 1 hour.

The bullet train helped save the railroad. Out of every 100 people going to work in Tokyo, fewer than 20 get there by car. In many U.S. cities, it's closer to 90 out of 100 taking cars. The bullet faces a new threat. Low-cost airlines promise to take people between major cities in Japan for less time and less money than the bullet. The Maglev might change that.

FAST FACT

The new Maglev line is predicted to cost more than $47 billion when it is completed in 2027.

Map of Japan

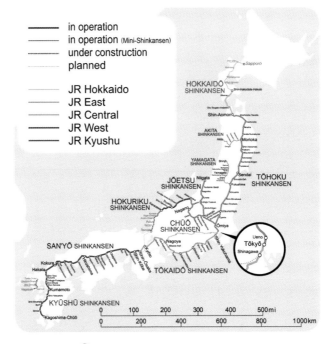

——	in operation
——	in operation (Mini-Shinkansen)
··········	under construction
··········	planned
——	JR Hokkaido
——	JR East
——	JR Central
——	JR West
——	JR Kyushu

HOKKAIDŌ SHINKANSEN

Sapporo

Shin-Hakodate-Hokuto

Shin-Aomori

AKITA SHINKANSEN

Akita

Morioka

YAMAGATA SHINKANSEN

Yamagata

Niigata

Sendai

TŌHOKU SHINKANSEN

JŌETSU SHINKANSEN

Fukushima

HOKURIKU SHINKANSEN

Nagano

Utsunomiya

CHŪŌ SHINKANSEN

Ōmiya

Ueno

Tōkyō

Shinagawa

Nagoya

SAN'YŌ SHINKANSEN

Kyoto

Shin-Osaka

TŌKAIDŌ SHINKANSEN

Kokura

Hakata

Kumamoto

KYŪSHŪ SHINKANSEN

Kagoshima-Chūō

0	100	200	300	400	500 mi
0	200	400	600	800	1000 km

How it Works

Shaped like a bullet to cut down on wind resistance, the train relies on electricity from overhead lines sent to each wheel from a motor connected to the axle. Communications and internet come from a series of antennae and transmitters.

Receiver Antennas

Transmitter Antenna

Repeater

Relay Antenna

What You Should Know

- The first Japanese Bullet Train arrived on October 1, 1964, just before the Olympics.

- The train is powered by electricity. It is sent to motors in the axles that connect to the wheels.

- It was the fastest train in the world.

- Today high-speed trains in China are faster. However, dozens of people have died in train accidents there. In Japan, no one has ever died from a train collision or a derailment.

- Soon high-speed trains in Japan will use magnets to reach speeds of more than 300 mph.

- The fastest high-speed trains in Japan reach 200 mph.

Glossary

axle
A rod that runs between two wheels

current
Flow of electricity

engineer
Person who designs projects like railroads or someone who operates a train

levitation
Making something rise up or hover

locomotive
A rail vehicle that is powered to pull rail cars

Find Out More

The Big Book of Trains, NY: DK Publishing, 2016.

Bankston, John. *Electric Trains and Trolleys.* (1880–Present). ML 2013.

Riggs, Kate. *Bullet trains*. Mankato, MN: Creative Education/Creative Paperbacks, 2015.

On the Internet

"High Speed Trains," DK Findout
https://www.dkfindout.com/us/transportation/history-trains/high-speed-trains/

Lori A. Selke, "Facts About Bullet Trains for Kids," *Arizona Central/USA Today*. **October 05, 2017**
https://getawaytips.azcentral.com/facts-about-bullet-trains-for-kids-12562488.html

"Train Technologies," Kids Web Japan
https://web-japan.org/kidsweb/hitech/shinkansen/shinkansen02.html

Index

About the Author

I was 13 the first time I took a train trip by myself. My mother told me stories about the fine dining cars she enjoyed as a girl. I was a bit disappointed. Although most trains in the U.S. are not elegant, they remain my favorite way to travel. They let you see the landscape and witness life in the backyards of strangers. In my teens, I traveled by train across the country from San Diego, California, to Brattleboro, Vermont. I took a rail trip from Capri to Rome in Italy. And more recently, I wrote the book *Electric Trains and Trolleys* for Mitchell Lane. I live in Miami Beach, Florida, where a high-speed train will soon connect to Orlando.